D1709992

The Coolest Inventor

Willis Haviland Carrier and His Air Conditioner

Alison and Stephen Eldridge

Enslow Elementary

an imprint of

Enslow Publishers, Inc.

40 Industrial Road
Box 398
Berkeley Heights, NJ 07922
USA

http://www.enslow.com

Enslow Elementary, an imprint of Enslow Publishers, Inc.

Enslow Elementary® is a registered trademark of Enslow Publishers, Inc.

Library of Congress Cataloging-in-Publication Data

Eldridge, Alison.
  The coolest inventor : Willis Haviland Carrier and his air conditioner / by Alison and Stephen Eldridge.
      pages cm — (Inventors at work!)
  Includes index.
  Summary: "Read about Willis Haviland Carrier's early life on a farm, his desire to go to college, and the
    creation of air conditioning"— Provided by publisher.
  ISBN 978-0-7660-4216-2
  1. Carrier, Willis Haviland, 1876-1950—Juvenile literature. 2. Air conditioning—History—Juvenile literature.
    3. Inventors—United States—Biography—Juvenile literature. I. Eldridge, Stephen. II. Title.
  TH140.C37E43 2014
  697.9'3092—dc23
  [B]
                              2012041458

Future editions:
Paperback ISBN: 978-1-4644-0375-0
EPUB ISBN: 978-1-4645-1207-0
Single-User PDF ISBN: 978-1-4646-1207-7
Multi-User PDF ISBN: 978-0-7660-5839-2

Printed in the United States of America
102013 Lake Book Manufacturing, Melrose Park, IL
10 9 8 7 6 5 4 3 2 1

To Our Readers: We have done our best to make sure all Internet Addresses in this book were active and appropriate when we went to press. However, the author and the publisher have no control over and assume no liability for the material available on those Internet sites or on other Web sites they may link to. Any comments or suggestions can be sent by e-mail to comments@enslow.com or to the address on the back cover.

♻ Enslow Publishers, Inc., is committed to printing our books on recycled paper. The paper in every book contains 10% to 30% post-consumer waste (PCW). The cover board on the outside of each book contains 100% PCW. Our goal is to do our part to help young people and the environment too!

Photo Credits: 1896 Illustrated General Catalogue of the Buffalo Horizontal and Upright Steam Engines, p. 16; © 1999 Artville, LLC, p. 6 (map); AP Images/Julio Cortez, p. 28; Big Cheese Photo/Thinkstock, p. 4; Carrier Corporation, pp. 10, 23, 25, 31, 34; Comstock/Thinkstock, p. 39; Dynamic Graphics/Thinkstock, p. 12; Image courtesy of Dorothy Goeller, p. 32; © iStockphoto.com/Jonathan Maddock, p. 36; iStockphoto.com/Thinkstock, pp. 18, 37; Library of Congress Prints and Photographs, pp. 14–15; Shutterstock.com, pp. 6 (farm), 7, 8, 11, 26, 40, 41, 42, 43; United States Patent Office, p. 20.

Cover Photos: Carrier Corporation

CONTENTS

What do you do to cool off? These kids use the pool, but it is easier to cool off in air-conditioning.

Growing Up Cool

Icky sticky! Does it get hot where you live? It feels great to walk into an air-conditioned room on a hot day and be greeted by a blast of cold air. But have you ever wondered who made it possible? You can thank Willis Carrier. He is the inventor of the air conditioner. Without him, millions of homes, classrooms, and offices would be too hot in the summer. Air-conditioning can even save lives!

When Willis Carrier was born, life was very different. He was born in Angola, New York, in 1876. In the 1870s, people didn't have many of the things we have today. There were no telephones. There were no cars or radios. There were definitely no computers or TVs!

Willis Carrier grew up on a farm in Angola, New York.

Not many people had lightbulbs or electricity. Of course there was no air-conditioning. Willis lived on a farm. There were not many children his own age to play with. You might think he was bored because he had no TV, movies, or video games. But Willis spent his free time making up problems to solve.

Growing Up on the Farm

Willis helped his father, Duane, clean and fix farm machines. As a young boy he even put together a whole tractor! He got his love of working with machines from his mother. Elizabeth Haviland Carrier was a schoolteacher. She also liked to fix things. She fixed the family sewing machine, alarm clock, and other things.

Young Willis came from a family that loved to fix things. His mother fixed many things in the home, including alarm clocks.

She also helped Willis with his schoolwork. When Willis was in school, he had trouble understanding math with fractions. His mother had him cut up apples to work out problems with them. This taught Willis that he could solve problems if he just broke them down into simple pieces. (And also that math can be delicious!)

Elizabeth died when Willis was only eleven years old. He never forgot what his mom told him: "Figure things out for yourself." In high school, Willis would often take longer than anyone else to do his homework. He wanted to be sure he had it perfect. Willis was lucky to go to high school. Many children in the 1800s stopped going before then.

School days were tough for Willis. On top of schoolwork, he had a lot to do! He began each day at 5:00 A.M., helping his father milk cows. Then he delivered the milk with a wagon. If there was snow, he had to use a sled! Then he went back home for breakfast

Willis Carrier (top left) and some high school classmates

and walked to school. After school, he would play until it was time to milk the cows again. Even if things were difficult, Willis was sure he could do anything if he tried hard enough.

When he finished high school, things were even harder. The farm was not making money. Even though most people did not, Willis had wanted to go to college. But he had to work to help his family make money. Luckily, Willis got a chance to study after all. If he hadn't, we may never have had air conditioners!

These containers are used to hold milk from a farm.

When Willis was growing up, people had all kinds of ways to keep cool. The oldest and most popular was very simple—build things underground! If you've ever gone into a basement when it's hot outside, you probably noticed that it was cooler down there. Heat from the sun has a hard time getting through the earth. So homes built into the ground don't get as warm in the summer. Another way to try to keep the hot sun out is to use thick, heavy walls. Making a building out of heavy brick can keep it cool.

Another way to keep cool is through evaporating water. This is how sweating cools your body down. When the water on a wet object starts to evaporate—turns into a gas—the object becomes cooler. Some people hang damp cloth in doorways. The air blowing into the room is cooled.

Others even wear wet clothes!

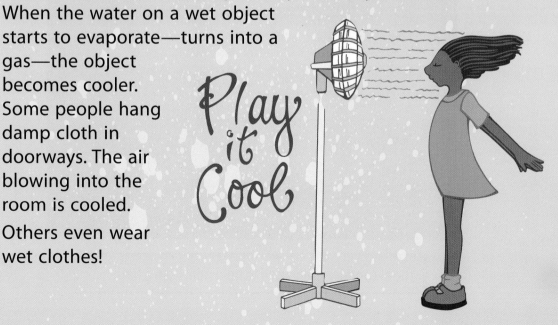

Play it Cool

Carrier, the Young Inventor

In 1896, Willis Carrier no longer had to help his family. His father married another woman. His stepmother sent him to live in Buffalo, New York, with one of her three adult sons. In Buffalo, he worked for his stepbrother's family. He also went to a new high school. Even though he'd finished school already, he had to go back in order to get into a good college. He entered a contest to win money for college. And he won! With that money and money from doing work, he was able to pay for college.

At Cornell University, Carrier studied electrical engineering. He was very smart. His classmates were impressed. One of his school friends said that not even the teachers could keep up with him! He was also good at sports like boxing, running, and rowing. Even though he was very busy, he got close to a young woman named Claire Seymour. They got married just a year after graduation.

Carrier studied electrical engineering at Cornell University.

Starting to Work

Because of his interest in electricity, Carrier hoped to work for a big company like General Electric. Instead, he went to work at the Buffalo Forge Company. At Buffalo Forge, Carrier learned about the problem of humidity.

Humidity is a word meaning "how much water is in the air." There is always some water in the air. It is not liquid water, like rain. It is water as a gas, like steam.

Carrier went to work at the Buffalo Forge Company.

Humidity can cause problems. If the air in a factory or warehouse is too humid, the water can cause damage. For example, in a factory that makes paper, the water will make the paper wet. Nobody can use wet paper!

A printing company in Brooklyn, New York, had hired Buffalo Forge to help them with a humidity problem. On the hot, humid days of summer, ink wouldn't always stick to paper right. Carrier needed to find a way to make sure the air in the printing plant was cool and dry. Carrier followed his mother's advice. He took this complicated problem and broke it into small parts.

Cool Air Gets Carrier Thinking

Carrier saw that when you cool air, the water in it turns from a gas into a liquid. Have you ever seen water drops appear out of nowhere on a glass? That's the water in the air turning to liquid when it touches the cold glass. Carrier just needed to figure out how cool to make the air. Then he needed to build a machine to do it. How would you tackle this problem?

When water in the air touches a cold glass, the water forms drops on the outside of the glass.

Carrier did research on temperature and humidity in the weather. This helped him figure out the right temperature for the air. Then he used coils of cold water to cool the air down to that temperature. His machine was a success! Carrier was soon asked to build more machines for other businesses.

After Carrier's success, Buffalo Forge set him up in a research laboratory. A research laboratory is a workshop for doing science experiments. In 1906, Carrier got his first patent for an "Apparatus for Treating Air." An apparatus is a machine, and this machine was a new way of keeping air cool and dry! It was the great-grandfather of the air conditioner you know today.

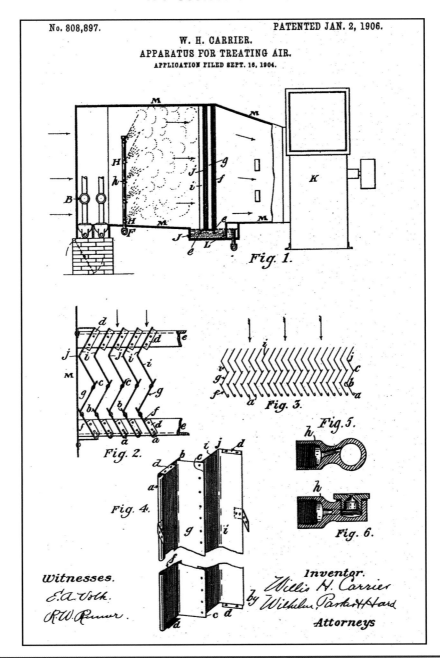

No. 808,897.
PATENTED JAN. 2, 1906.
W. H. CARRIER.
APPARATUS FOR TREATING AIR.
APPLICATION FILED SEPT. 16, 1904.

Fig. 1.
Fig. 2.
Fig. 3.
Fig. 4.
Fig. 5.
Fig. 6.

Witnesses.
E. A. Volk.
R. W. Renner.

Inventor.
Willis H. Carrier.
by Wilhelm, Parker & Hard
Attorneys

A patent has drawings of an invention and details that show the invention is unique.

Patents

When someone is given a patent, it means the government says they are the creator of an invention. An invention is any new machine or way of doing things that nobody has thought of before. You can make inventions, too!

If someone has a patent for an invention, no one else can say they invented it. It also means that only the real inventor can sell the invention. Anyone else who wants to build and sell the same thing will need to get permission. This usually means paying the inventor some money in exchange for permission to sell the invention. Patents don't last forever. Usually, they last twenty years. After that, anyone can use the inventor's work.

Patents help people share their knowledge. To get a patent, inventors have to make their invention public. They have to let everyone know how it works. Without a patent, inventors might keep their inventions a secret so no one else could make them. With a patent, no one else is allowed to make the invention. But everyone is free to learn about it!

Climate Control

In 1906, the Chronicle Cotton Mills of Belmont, North Carolina, was the first to install Willis Carrier's air-treating machine. It was the first central air-conditioning system. Carrier's invention could make the air drier by spraying water into it!

Carrier's invention sprayed a mist of cold water into the air. If the air was very warm and humid, the cold water would make the air cooler. When humid air gets cold, some of the water separates from the air, like the drops of water that form on a glass. The air could actually become drier than it was before. Carrier worked hard to figure out how to keep the air as cool, warm, humid, or dry as his customers needed it.

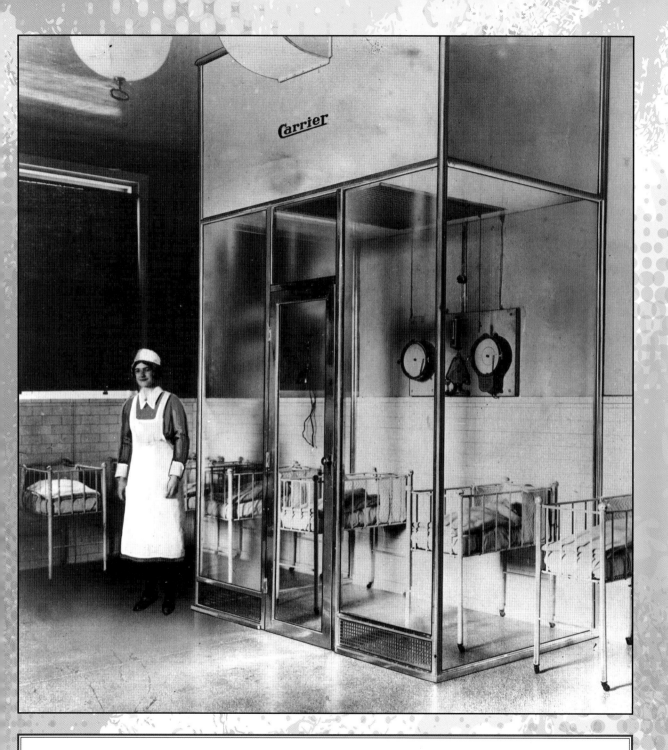

In 1914, Carrier's air-conditioning at the Allegheny Hospital in Pittsburgh, Pennsylvania, helped cool the incubator room for babies. The temperature in an incubator is comfortable for newborns.

Air-Conditioning Gets Popular

More and more businesses came to Buffalo Forge for their air-conditioning. At first, these businesses wanted dry, cool air to make their products better. Companies that made cloth wanted air conditioners to keep their cloth from getting musty or shrinking. A company that made medicine was another early customer. The Celluloid Company, which made film, came soon after. Because of Willis Carrier's invention, we have better clothing, medicine, and even movies! Department stores, soap factories, bakeries, and all kinds of other buildings all wanted air conditioners.

In 1907, the Buffalo Forge Company was so busy that they created a new company. The new company handled all of the requests for air-conditioning. They called it the Carrier Air Conditioning Company of America. Willis Carrier was the company's vice president.

Willis Carrier

Modern Air Conditioners

Carrier's machines and his research paved the way for future air conditioners. Carrier and others continued making new ways to keep air cool and dry for many years. Air conditioners today are a little different from the ones Carrier first invented. They use gases called refrigerants to cool down air instead of using water. But they still rely on Carrier's research and ideas.

This modern air conditioner cools an entire house.

Successes and Struggles

Over the next few years, Willis Carrier worked hard to build the Carrier Air Conditioning Company. Sadly, his wife, Claire, died in 1912. Carrier remarried just a year later. His second wife, Jennie Tifft Martin, had two children. Carrier adopted them as his own.

In 1914, World War I began. Because of the war, Buffalo Forge had to make cuts to its business. At the time, the Carrier Air Conditioning Company was a small part of their business. Willis Carrier took his ideas and several of his workers to form a new company. In 1915, he created the Carrier Engineering Corporation.

Air-conditioning at Madison Square Garden in New York City lets people ice skate indoors!

Getting Comfortable

Before, air-conditioning had only been used to help companies produce better goods. Making people more comfortable on hot days was just a bonus! In the 1920s Carrier went to work on a new goal: "comfort" air-conditioning. The Carrier Engineering Corporation put air-conditioning systems in hotels and movie theaters. One of Carrier's biggest customers was Madison Square Garden, a stadium for sports and events in New York City.

Madison Square Garden opened in 1925. It used Carrier's inventions for two reasons. First, it used air-conditioning to keep its customers cool. Second, it used Carrier's inventions to create indoor ice for people to skate on. The Carrier Engineering Corporation helped athletes play hockey!

New inventions helped Carrier stay successful. The most important was a new kind of machine for refrigerating air. The "centrifugal chiller" was smaller and more powerful than older machines. A man named L. Logan Lewis came up with a new invention to fan cool air around rooms. These machines helped Carrier make big buildings, such as Madison Square Garden, cooler.

Unfortunately, the 1930s were a difficult time for Willis Carrier. In 1930, Carrier Engineering and two other companies were put together into one company. The new company was called the Carrier Corporation. Like many companies, the Carrier Corporation struggled in the 1930s because of the Great Depression. The Great Depression was a time when many people were poor and many businesses closed. In 1939 Carrier's second wife, Jennie, died.

Helping in the War Effort

Carrier married for a third time in 1941, to Mary Elizabeth Wise. That year, the United States entered World War II. The Carrier Corporation helped the war

The first centrifugal chiller was announced in 1922.

"Now let me at 'em!...

After a meal like that I'm ready to lick my weight in wildcats. Hurry up, soldier, let's go!"

Good food ... 6,000 miles from Home

SURE HE'S UP CLOSE. The big guns are barking, machine guns rattling. There's a lot of action and not far away. But he eats. In the far Pacific or in the land of the midnight sun your boy gets plenty of good energy-building food.

Refrigeration and air conditioning are doing a job. Foods are rushed across land in Carrier refrigerated trucks . . . across seas in Carrier equipped ships . . . and stored at bases where the perishables depend on the reliability of refrigerating machines thousands of miles away from a repair shop.

Meats are produced in packing plants air conditioned by Carrier. Vegetables and fruits are dehydrated to conserve precious shipping space. By removing moisture from the air, Carrier Air Conditioning keeps them rich in vitamins and food values. The soldier's coffee is fresher . . . his cereal crisper . . . through Carrier control of temperature, humidity, and air cleanliness during production.

Aloft, Afloat, Ashore—
this is an AIR CONDITIONED War

In many other ways, the men and women of Carrier are contributing to the war effort. By controlling "indoor weather", aircraft plants turn out better engines . . . blast furnaces produce more iron . . . precision plants make range-finders and bomb-sights of unmatched accuracy. The fact is that air conditioning is a weapon, new and powerful—and one that is helping to win this war.

Today Carrier is applying its facilities and skill to war production. Tomorrow Carrier will build better products for peace.

The Navy "E", one of the U. S. Navy's most coveted honors, was awarded to Carrier Corporation for excellence in war production

Carrier Air Conditioning

Carrier Corporation, Syracuse, New York
WEATHERMAKERS TO THE WORLD

THE SATURDAY EVENING POST · JUNE 27, 1942

Prepared by

Refrigeration helped feed the troops during World War II.

effort by air-conditioning factories that made goods for the war. They also refrigerated food to feed troops thousands of miles from home. After World War II ended in 1945, Americans had more money to spend. For the first time, many people could afford to have air-conditioning in their homes. The Carrier Corporation was growing again.

The 1939 New York World's Fair was a huge display of new inventions and ideas. The motto of the Fair was "Building a Better Tomorrow." This is something Willis Carrier had always worked to do. The Carrier Corporation was one of the many companies that gave a demonstration at the Fair. They built a huge air-conditioned igloo and showed Carrier's new inventions for cooling homes. They also showed new, more powerful refrigerators. They showed air conditioners that could fit in a person's home. Over a million people came to see the show!

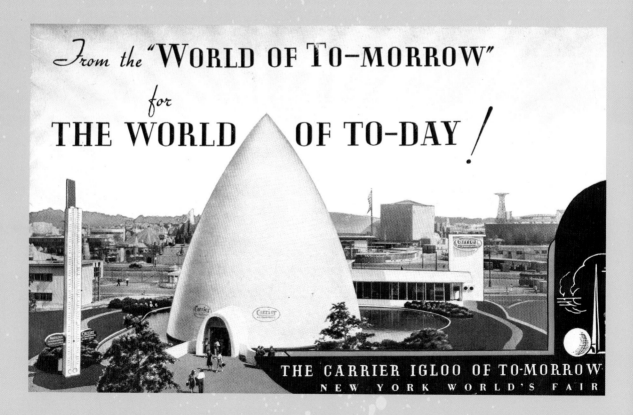

A Cool Legacy

In the late 1940s, Willis Carrier began suffering from a serious heart condition. He died on October 9, 1950. However, Carrier's amazing inventions are still changing the world today. Central air-conditioning can keep very large buildings from getting stuffy. Air conditioners can help keep air clean and dry. This is important for building parts of computers and other electronic parts. Air-conditioning even helps keep hospitals clean so diseases don't spread!

Through the 1950s, more and more people started putting air conditioners in their homes. Carrier's invention started to get popular in other areas as well.

Ocean liners and buses had been using air-conditioning for years. But air-conditioning in cars had not been very successful. That changed in 1953. New air conditioners for cars were easier to use. More car companies started using the new air conditioners in the cars they sold. By the 1970s, air-conditioning came in most new cars.

Since the 1950s, air-conditioning has become more popular outside of the United States. This has led

Air-conditioning in airplanes makes flights more comfortable.

All cars now offer air-conditioning.

people to think about how air-conditioning affects the world. Some kinds of gases that were used to chill air, called CFCs (short for chlorofluorocarbons), can hurt the environment. These gases are no longer used in air conditioners. Running an air conditioner also takes a lot of power. The electricity air conditioners use often comes from burning oil, coal, or other fuels that cause pollution. Companies like the Carrier Corporation do research to try to make new models that use less energy.

Next time you are in an air-conditioned room, you will know whom to thank. Because of Willis Carrier, people are happier and safer today. And inventors continue to work with Carrier's invention to make even more great things. Maybe one of those inventors will be you!

Today's air-conditioning makes life comfortable!

So you want to be an inventor? You can do it! First, you need a terrific idea.

Got a Problem? No Problem!

Many inventions begin when someone thinks of a great solution to a problem. One cold day in 1994, ten-year-old K. K. Gregory was building a snow fort. Soon, she had snow between her mittens and her coat sleeve. Her wrists were cold and wet. She found some scraps of fabric around the house and used them to make a tube that would fit around her wrist. She cut a thumb hole in the tube to make a kind of fingerless glove and called it a "Wristie." By wearing mittens over her new invention, her wrists stayed nice and warm when she played outside. Today, the Wristie business is booming.

Now it's your turn. Maybe, like K. K. Gregory, you have an idea for something new that would make your life better or easier. Perhaps you can think of a way to improve an everyday item. Twelve-year-old Becky Schroeder became one of the youngest people ever to receive a U.S. patent after she invented a glow-in-the-dark clipboard that allowed people to write in the dark. Do you like to play sports or board games? James Naismith, inspired by a game he used to play as a boy, invented a new game he called basketball.

Let your imagination run wild. You never know where it will take you.

Research It!

Okay, you have a terrific idea for an invention. Now what?

First, you will want to make sure that nobody else has thought of your idea. You

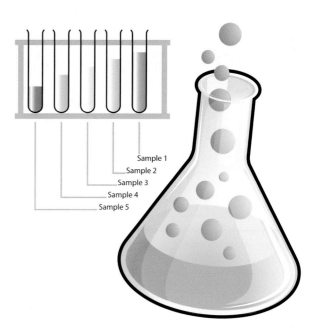

Sample 1
Sample 2
Sample 3
Sample 4
Sample 5

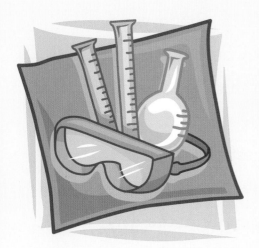

wouldn't want to spend hours developing your new invention only to find that someone else beat you to it. Check out Google Patents (see Learn More for the Web site address), which can help you find out whether your idea is original.

Bring It to Life!

If no one else has thought of your idea, congratulations! Write it down in a notebook. Date and initial every entry you make. If you file a patent for your invention later, this will help you prove that you were the first to think of it. The most important thing about this logbook is that pages cannot be added or subtracted. You can buy a bound notebook at any office supply store.

Draw several different pictures of your invention in your logbook. Try sketching views from above, below, and to the side. Show how big each part of your invention should be.

Build a model. Don't be discouraged if it doesn't work at first. You may have to experiment with different designs and materials. That's part of the fun! Take pictures of everything, and tape them into your logbook. Try your invention out on your friends and family. If they have any suggestions to make it better, build another model. Perfect your invention, and give it a clever name.

Patent It!

Do you want to sell your invention? You'll want to apply for a patent. Holding a patent to your invention means that no one else can make, use, or sell your invention in the United States without your permission. It prevents others from making money off your idea. You will definitely need an adult to help you apply for a patent. It can be a complicated and expensive process. But if you think that people will want to buy your invention, it is well worth it. Good luck!

TIMELINE

1876: Willis Haviland Carrier is born in Angola, New York, on November 26.

1901: Graduates from Cornell University.

1902: Marries his first wife, Claire Seymour.

1902: Designs the first modern air conditioner.

1906: Gets his first patent.

1912: Death of his first wife, Claire.

1913: Marries his second wife, Jennie Tifft Martin.

1915: Starts the Carrier Engineering Corporation.

1930: Creation of the Carrier Corporation.

1939: Death of his second wife, Jennie.

1941: Marries his third wife, Mary Elizabeth Wise.

1950: Dies in New York City on October 7.

WORDS TO KNOW

air-conditioning—Controlling the temperature and humidity in a certain space.

centrifugal—Moving away from a central point.

CFCs (chlorofluorocarbons)—Chemicals used for cooling that can be harmful to the environment.

electrical engineering—Building machines that use electricity.

evaporate—To change from a liquid to a gas.

Great Depression—A time in American history (1929–1941) when many people were poor and many businesses closed.

humidity—The amount of water vapor in air.

patent—A document from the government that says that someone is the inventor of something. Nobody else may make or sell that invention without the inventor's permission.

refrigerant—A gas used to make things cool.

ventilation—A way to bring fresh air into a space.

Books

Books

Macauley, David. *The New Way Things Work*. Boston: Houghton Mifflin Company, 1998.

Platt, Richard. *Eureka! Great Inventions and How They Happened*. Boston: Kingfisher, 2003.

Romanek, Trudee. *Switched On, Flushed Down, Tossed Out: Investigating the Hidden Workings of Your Home*. Toronto: Annick Press, 2005.

Ticotsky, Alan. *Science Giants: Earth and Space*. Tucson, Arizona: Good Year Books, 2006.

Web Sites

Google Patents.
  <http://google.com/patents>

**The Father of Cool: "Willis Haviland Carrier.
  The History of Air Conditioning."**
  <http://inventors.about.com/library/weekly/
  aa081797.htm>

INDEX